The Urban Educator's Survival Guide:
School Teachers in Violent Classrooms

Dennis Nappi II

Published by Service of Change, LLC

ISBN: 978 0 9911375 4 1

For additional free resources, visit www.ServiceOfChange.com/Teachers

Contents

Introduction

Today, the Internet and social media feeds are plagued with hundreds of violent cell-phone fight videos. Many of these videos are set in school classrooms and often depict teachers caught in compromising situations for either their attempted intervention or lack thereof. Because of these videos, several teachers have lost their jobs. Because of these fights, both students and teachers have suffered serious injuries. In today's educational environment, a violent outburst is an inevitable part of anyone's teaching career, yet teachers have very little education and training on how to respond to such an incident. They are left unprepared and uninformed as to how to address a violent threat in their classroom.

During my first year as a teacher, after witnessing several fights during the first few weeks of school, I asked my administrator what I was supposed to do when a fight broke out. He smiled, shook his head, and told me: "Mr. Nappi, you're f**ked if you do and you're f**ked if you don't." Those words have never left me, and I have spent my entire career trying to find not only a better explanation, but a better way to address violent outbursts. Using my experiences as a soldier and police officer, I have tried to incorporate multiple methods to protect students and staff when addressing a violent incident. What I have found works best is a combination of education, preparation, planning, and prevention. If you have read the first edition of *The Urban Educator's Survival Guide: 7 Proven Strategies From a Successful School Teacher's Classroom,* then you will already have many of the tools you need in place to build a solid foundation in preventing violence. This guide takes your classroom management to the next level and aims to prepare you to address violence after all attempts have been made to prevent it.

When violence erupts in your classroom, will you know what to do? Are you prepared to address a threat directed against you or your students? Are you prepared to handle yourself appropriately, safely, and professionally while still protecting your job? This guide is designed to help you for the unfortunate, yet probable event that you find yourself engaged in a violent altercation in your classroom.

Planning & Preparation

When I was in the police academy, my defensive tactics instructor made a statement that has never left me, and for good reason. He stated that in a crisis situation, we fall back onto our highest level of training. This means that if something happens causing your adrenaline to spike, you will not have time to think about what you are going to do. Your mind and body will simply react to the crisis-causing stimuli. If you do not have any training, you may experience panic, freeze, or scramble to make a poor decision that could cost you your job or bring harm to yourself and the people around you. For this reason, my instructor stated that training and preparation are essential components when addressing any violent outburst.

Just as a teacher prepares a lesson plan for the day's activities, each teacher should also have an action plan in the event of a violent crisis. It is always better to spend time thinking and planning for an incident before it happens than it is to try to develop a plan once the fists start flying.

But how does a teacher plan for violence? A good starting point would be with the school's emergency plan, rules, and regulations. Many schools have some sort of document that explains, at a minimum, the consequences for fighting and the procedure for stopping that violent action. Review that document and make a list of any questions you may have.

Some important things to consider in your plan:

1. *What is your responsibility when a fight breaks out? Are you expected to intervene, observe, control the crowd, or call for help?*
2. *What communication method is used to call for help? Should you use shouting, phones, or radios?*
3. *Is there a crisis response team in place? What is the procedure for activating them?*
4. *Is there any training available for you?*

If you find yourself in a school without a written emergency plan, start asking questions. Ask your administrator and ask your colleagues what your role is when violence breaks out. Be sure to document your conversations and the information given to you with dates and times. (We will discuss the importance of documentation in a later chapter).

Once you have reviewed your schools plan and asked any questions you have, it is time to develop *your* plan, which starts with a self-assessment. You need to take some time to reflect and evaluate your own capabilities and feelings toward addressing a violent outburst. Consider the following:

1. *What is your current physical condition? Are you a marathon runner or more comfortable on the couch?*
2. *Do you have any training? Maybe you have a background in martial arts, or grew up in a violent neighborhood and are accustomed to violence. However, you may not be and it is important to recognize this because when you witness your first fight you may find it extremely difficult to watch.*
3. *What are your personal and moral beliefs and feelings about violence? It is important to understand your own feelings about violence so you can determine which level of intervention you are comfortable with.*

Once you have completed a self-assessment, you should be conscious of your capabilities and limitations. It is now time to develop your plan. While you are drafting your violence-intervention plan, you must be sure to keep your plan in compliance with the already pre-established school policies. If the school states that under no circumstances is a teacher to put hands on a student for whichever reason, then make sure your plan does not include flying ninja kicks as one of your intervention strategies to break up a fight.

A sample violence-intervention plan may look something like this:

Step 1 – Call for Help. As a police officer, I was always taught that no matter what I was doing while on the job, the first thing I absolutely needed to do was to let dispatch know where I was. That way, if something went wrong, and dispatch stopped hearing from me, they would know where to send help. As a teacher, this is of the utmost importance. Once you realize a fight is imminent, or even before, call for help even if the only words you get out are your room number. People can't help you if they don't know where you are. If you are not near your phone or radio, have a trusted student make that call. (We will talk more about this in our training section).

Step 2 – Evaluate your surroundings and the situation. Your first priority is to ensure your own safety, then the safety of your students, and lastly the safety of those fighting. Take note of the number of bystanders, the number and size of combatants, the presence of weapons, the number of staff present, and environmental factors such as desks and tables. These should all be considered as you begin your intervention plan.

Step 3 – Crowd control. You want to move all uninvolved students away from the fight. Have them go into the hallway or simply to the other side of the room. They are not going to want to leave the scene, but you need to make an attempt by giving commands to do so. Do NOT put your hands on students or start shoving them. Use your *voice* and give clear directions: "Move to the back of the room NOW!" or simply, "Get BACK!" are commands that work well.

Step 4 – Move objects that can harm the combatants and staff. Start moving desks out of the way, and pick up any sharp or blunt objects that can be used as weapons. Plan ahead of time where you are going to place them.

Step 5 – Give clear commands to the combatants to stop fighting. "Break it up! Stop Fighting!" Continue to shout these phrases throughout the entire duration of the fight. If the incident is recorded, it will show you making efforts to stop the fight and regain control.

Step 6 – This is being recorded. Remember, cell phones will be recording everything that happens, to include your actions or lack thereof. If the school tries to hold you liable, the video will show everything you did. Be mindful of your actions and words, as everything you do can be used against you, even if it is taken out of context.

Step 7 – Inform and delegate. When help finally arrives, you are the authority with the most knowledge about the situation. You have command over the scene and those coming to help you may need direction. If you are having issues with crowd control, tell the staff to move the crowd back. Be sure to identify who you are speaking to by name so there is no confusion. "John, move these students to the hallway." You also want to give a quick update to those who are actually breaking up the fight. If you are going to be involved in separating the students, be sure to communicate your plan. "Dave, you grab the student on the bottom and take him to the hallway. I will take the other student to the back of the room." As the situation unfolds, continue to communicate. Be sure to notify your team of the presence of blood or weapons by simply shouting it out. "Blood!" or "Careful, he has a pencil in his right hand." Communication is very important when trying to break up a fight and can help ensure the safety of all involved.

Most of these steps you will do simultaneously. When a fight breaks out, you will immediately call for help or have a student do so. Then as you are shouting for your students to clear the area, you are also moving desks and potential weapons out of the way. In between shouts for the uninvolved students to move away, you are also shouting for the combatants to break it up. This whole incident takes seconds to unfold and can appear like chaos. However, if you have a plan, regardless of how terrifying it may seem, you will be able to dissect that chaos one step at a time as you work to end the incident. Following a plan offers a sense of inner calmness and reassurance when facing what seems to be an uncontrollable situation. Take the time to develop your plan and when the time comes to enact that plan you will realize exactly what is meant by the statement: "an ounce of preparation is worth a pound of cure."

Training

As I stated in the previous chapter, in a crisis situation we fall back to our highest level of training. Once your plan is developed, it's time to start practicing your plan because without practice and training, your plan is nothing more than a piece of paper that won't be any good to you when a fight erupts. You may remember a few of the steps or only that a plan exists, but you will not naturally react in accordance with your plan. Practice, practice, practice!

When a fight breaks out in the classroom, the goal of the teacher is to ensure the safety of all students. As teachers, we always aim to prepare ourselves for every possible classroom scenario, and our goals as educators is to prepare our students for life in the real world. So why not take the time to also prepare our students for addressing violence in the classroom? By this statement, I do not mean we need to teach our students how to fight. In my classroom, right around the time I am reviewing our school's emergency procedures, I hold a discussion about a classroom fight. I tell my students it is unacceptable to fight in my classroom and I often share examples of the injuries I have witnessed. I then explain to them what I will be doing if a fight breaks out in the classroom and I run through my entire plan.

I tell my students that I will immediately call for help so that other teachers, administrators, and police will be coming to the scene. This lets them know I have zero tolerance for violence in my classroom. But it is also an opportunity for me to add: "Sometimes I may not be able to get to a phone. I may ask you to pick up my phone and call (12345). Please tell them there is a fight and give them our room number." I give them clear instructions so they can be equally prepared if I give them this task because I want their highest level of training to include calling for help. I then tell them that I may also send some of them next door to get another teacher to come help. I also tell them that they will be expected to move away from the fight, and any resistance to my commands to move away will be dealt with through official school consequences.

I continue through my plan, explaining each step. "I want you all to understand this. I also want you to understand that if I shout at you during a situation like this, it is only because of adrenaline and I mean you no disrespect." I elaborate on this because I want my students to understand that I may be shouting to reestablish order and not to disrespect them. I have seen student bystanders become combatants because the teachers trying to clear a safe space had aggressive tones. "Please forgive me in advance," I apologize, "and if my shouting really offends you, please feel free to come tell me about it once things are calm and I guarantee I will apologize then as well." With these statements, I am trying to establish trust with my students. I do not want them to view me as a threat, and I need them to understand that my actions are intended only to protect their own safety, to include those who may be fighting.

Because I have taken the time to have these discussions and prepare my students, I have found that during violent altercations I have been able to pull combatants away from a fight without that violence being redirected toward me. Students understand that I am there to help and not a threat to them. On the contrary, however, I have intervened in fights where the students did not know who I was and found myself being attacked as a result. However, regardless of my relationship with the student, I will never let my guard down until I have safely escorted that student away from the fight and they are no longer exhibiting threatening signs of aggression. Trust goes a long way, but there will always be that one student who decides to take a swing.

Once my students are prepared, I need to make sure I am ready to address any violent outbursts in my classroom. In order to prepare myself for violence, I rely on what I consider to be one of the most valuable training tools used by police officers everywhere: My imagination. As a police officer and a teacher, I have found that my greatest method of preparation for violence has been to mentally role play countless scenarios. I am constantly imagining different events and running through the execution of my entire plan with each one. If I am teaching in the front of the room, I imagine a fight breaking out in the back or the hallway. I then run through all of my steps – I imagine directing a student to call for help and another to notify the teacher next door. I visualize myself moving desks out of the way as I am shouting commands and I actually scan the room for anything that can be used as a weapon so I know what to grab first if a fight really breaks out. Sometimes, I visualize these events on my drive to work, or when I am walking down the hallway, and not a day goes by where I don't envision my response to at least one violent scenario.

As cops, we were taught about muscle memory which refers to our ability to react a certain way without any thought whatsoever. Much like we instinctively pull our hands away from a hot stove, we can also train ourselves to instinctively block a punch. In order to train our muscles and our bodies to react without thinking, however, we need to repeat these movements over 500 times. With life being as busy as it is, and our profession being focused on education and not violence, most teachers don't have the time to run through their violence-intervention plans twice, let alone 500 times. But since we are training our "brain muscle" to follow a set of procedures, I have found great success in mental role playing. In my mind, I frequently run through the plan, and since I am using my imagination, I incorporate every possible variable I can think of so *if* that scenario plays out I will have some level of preparation for it. As a police officer, I ran these scenarios *constantly:* while driving to a complaint, while talking to a suspect, or even while grocery shopping. I was constantly assessing my surroundings and asking myself "what would I do if…" As teachers, this level of preparation may be the only training you receive and could offer you the preparation needed to prevent a serious injury from a violent conflict.

Documentation

One of the most important, yet often forgotten, responses to a violent classroom altercation is the ability to accurately document the events that took place. A properly documented report can ultimately protect you in the event of a lawsuit because it will contain the necessary elements you may soon forget if you fail to write them down.

When writing your report, remember to include "just the facts," as the saying goes. There is no place for opinions and feelings in an incident report as they are nothing more than speculation. Simply write the facts and what you observed in chronological order.

Here are some documentation guidelines:

1. *Identify the date, time, and exact location of the incident.*
2. *Identify yourself by name and title.*
3. *Identify the suspects (combatants) involved by name, grade, and title (student).*
4. *Identify witnesses by name and title (teacher or student).*

5. *Explain the situation from beginning to end. Start with the antecedent to the violence, whether it was an argument, action, or if it stemmed from outside the school. Follow, chronologically, everything that happened. If you witnessed Student A punch Student B, state that in your report. "Student A punched Student B in the face 3 times."*

6. *Describe your actions. Let your reader know everything you did to intervene. This can be very important in court later. Remember, you are most likely being filmed so be honest about your actions. "I gave commands for the students to 'stop fighting,' and to 'get back.'" If you had to put your hands on a student, explain why: "In order to prevent Student A from further injuring Student B, I attempted to move Student A to a safe location by grabbing Student A's right arm and pulling him away."*

7. *Lastly, try to anticipate any questions an attorney, administrator, or anyone else would ask you and include that information in your report. If you didn't call for help, state that you were unable to call for help because you could not reach your phone, but you did "direct Student C to run next door*

> *for assistance." This statement will prevent your boss or an attorney from asking you the question of "why didn't you call for help," which can insinuate to a review board that you somehow failed to act appropriately. The more thorough you are, the less questions authorities will have, the less time you may have to spend in the hot seat defending your actions.*

Below is a sample incident report. I prefer to write in the third person because I think it sounds more formal and less personal, however, first person is also acceptable.

On 24 March 2014, at approximately 11:30 a.m., Teacher Dennis Nappi II, at ABC School, was in the hallway in front of room 821 when Mr. Nappi heard shouts coming from within room 821. Mr. Nappi entered the classroom and observed Student Frankie Fangs shouting "don't call me names," at Student David Danger. David then raised both fists and stated "I'm going to punch you," to Frankie. Frankie took a step back as David lunged forward and punched Frankie in the face two times. Frankie fell to the ground and kicked David's right leg with Frankie's left foot. David and Frankie then both continued to punch and kick one-another an unknown number of times on the head and body.

As Mr. Nappi entered the classroom, Mr. Nappi directed Student Sally Sweetheart to "call for help." Sally ignored Mr. Nappi's request and did not make a call for help. Student Jane Justice then ran next door and notified Teacher Steven Savior.

Mr. Nappi shouted 3 times for all students to move back as Mr. Nappi moved desks away from the two fighting students. Mr. Savior entered the room and both Mr. Savior and Mr. Nappi shouted on at least 4 occasions each for the students to "stop fighting." The students failed to comply with either teachers' commands. In an attempt to prevent injury to David and Frankie, Mr. Nappi grabbed David by David's left leg and pulled him away from Frankie. David then stood up and walked into the hallway with Mr. Nappi. Mr. Savior grabbed Frankie's right arm and pulled him away from David toward the back of the room where Frankie was instructed by Mr. Savior to sit in a chair. Frankie complied with Mr. Savior's request.

Mr. Pal, the school principal, then arrived at Room 821 and Mr. Pal and Mr. Savior both escorted David and Frankie to the main office for further investigation without incident.

After the fight is over, the report writing process is an excellent way to reflect on what happened. I often take some time before I start writing to review the sequence of events with other staff members who were involved to make sure we have an accurate description of what happened. Each staff member involved should submit a report based on their own actions and observations. This gives multiple perspectives of the same incident and lends credibility to your report, which can also protect students and teachers in the even that false accusations are made. Having a post-fight discussion with colleagues is also a great opportunity for an After-Action Review, which we will discuss in greater detail in the following chapter. If you suspect a complaint may be filed against you, however, be sure to review your report with a union representative before submitting it to your administrator.

In this day and age, documentation is one of the greatest forms of protection a teacher has against accusations, administrators, and law suits. As mentioned in an earlier chapter, let's assume your administrator informed you there was not a policy to address fighting and he denied your requests for training. If you documented this conversation, it could prove to be a key piece of information if the boss tries to fire you months later for trying to break up a fight. I usually try to capture these conversations electronically which is why my preferred method of documentation is through my company email. I will either ask my boss directly through email (and blind copy myself), or, if the conversation took place by another means I will email a follow-up question and reference the bosses initial statement in my email. This way you will still have a record of the boss's acknowledgement of your documented discussion. If the email option is not available, I also keep a simple log that lists the date, time, and any relevant information that needs to be documented. For example:

05 25 14 at 2:00 p.m. – I spoke with Principal Pal today and asked if we had an altercation policy. Mr. Pal advised we didn't have one. I asked if I could attend crisis intervention training, and Mr. Pal advised I was unable to do so.

Remember to make copies of all of your documentation and keep them in a secure place outside of the school (where officials will not have access to them). If you can get signatures on your incident reports, this will also prove beneficial in case your reports get "lost" when an investigation is launched. Again, emailing these reports and blind copying yourself is a great way to prove you submitted your report.

After-Action Review

During my time in the military, I found some of my greatest learning opportunities came during our frequent After-Action Reviews (AAR). The idea behind an AAR is to create a reflection period after an incident. This reflection allows the participants to evaluate their actions and improve their overall performance for future events. Although it is a time to be critical, it is not a time to criticize *individuals* for mistakes they made. The goal is to learn from mistakes and not to punish for errors in judgment.

The components of an AAR are simple. After a fight, set aside a time for the staff involved to have a discussion. It doesn't have to be formal. Once everyone is together, have a discussion on the following, giving each member an opportunity to talk:

1. ***Review the facts of the incident.*** *This is not a time to brag and share war stories. Stick to the facts and review the entire incident so team members who may have only witnessed a portion of the incident can be brought up to speed and learn what*

everyone did so they are better prepared for future events.

2. **Describe what went well**. *Have the team members list the actions that were done well. The goal is to develop a list of things the team would like to sustain and would do again should another incident arise. For example: "It was great that Mr. Nappi asked a student to call for help. We should always make sure we call for help."*

3. **Describe what could have been done better.** *This is a time for serious reflection without blame. The goal is to learn from mistakes. For example: "When the students were on the ground, there was a pen lying next to David. We should try to be aware of objects on the ground that can be used as weapons and next time try to kick it away." Again, the hope is that the next time a teacher is intervening in a fight he will be sure to look for any potential weapons that are on the ground. The emphasis should always be kept on learning from mistakes to improve your response during the next incident and never on blaming individual members for mistakes made. Leave that to the administrators.*

Once the AAR is complete, staff can then modify or adjust their plans to better address future problems. If you have a supportive administrator, you may consider presenting these ideas to him or her to enact a school-wide policy.

One final component of the AAR would involve the student reflection. As teachers, our goal is to provide support and education to our students. We are supposed to prepare them for life in the real world, and having a discussion after their engagement in a violent incident is an excellent opportunity for growth and learning. If you've read the *7 Proven Strategies from a School Teacher's Classroom,* this would be a great way to build and maintain rapport with your students. Keep in mind, school policy may dictate that a guidance counselor or administrator needs to hold these types of discussions, and in these situations I have requested to be present during the meeting and have never been denied. This discussion has several goals:

1. *It allows the student to have a voice and express any concerns he or she has. Sometimes during these meetings I have*

learned of more pending violence and been able to stop it before it happened.

2. *It is a time for staff to review school policy with the student. I like to remind the student of the rules and ask "What could you have done differently?" This allows the student to reflect on his actions and hopefully make better choices when presented with a similar situation in the future.*

3. *This conversation shows the student you still care. So many of our students are acting out violently because they are emotionally scarred. They have a history of neglect and sometimes abuse and are used to being rejected by authority when they step out of line. By having a compassionate conversation and stressing that you are still there to support the student, you can reinforce the student's trust in you.*

4. *It is also a time to issue consequences. Sometimes the consequences are issued prior to this meeting, immediately following the incident. If a suspension is issued, the meeting may take place upon the students return. Regardless, during this meeting it is appropriate to discuss the consequences and*

> *the reason why they were issued. Have the student explain why such a consequence was issued to demonstrate his understanding. Also, explain to the student that this incident is in the past and he has a fresh start. Remember, the goal is to teach our students, not to continually punish and reprimand them for mistakes made in the past.*

I have found these discussions can be beneficial for all parties involved. The ultimate goal is the prevention of future violent outbursts, and these conversations can be a major step toward achieving your violence-prevention endeavors.

Situational Awareness

Situational awareness is one's ability to perceive things going on in his surrounding environment. When you walk down the street, what do you see? I'm sure we all see cars and people. But is there more information available to your senses that could help keep you safe? When I walk down the street, I not only see cars and people, I always take note of the street names, cross streets, and addresses in case I need to call for help. Furthermore, I notice dark alleys, open doors, and large vans, all of which are places where potential threats could be hiding. When I see people, I notice clothing and hands. Could they conceal weapons in any parts of their clothing, or are they holding something that could harm me in their hands? When running my detective agency, I armed myself with all of this available information and was able to successfully navigate some very dangerous sections of Philadelphia on my own without incident. As I tell my students: "Street smarts is not knowing how to fight. It is knowing how not to get into a fight."

As a teacher, situational awareness is equally important. We need to pay attention to our students and our surrounding environments. If we watch close enough, we too can use that information to identify a problem before it becomes violent and intervene. Here is an example:

While teaching a class you notice one of your students is staring off into space. This is not a normal behavior for this student. He is holding a pencil in his hand and squeezing it so hard that his knuckles are turning white. His breathing is heavy and you can see his chest heaving up and down with each breath. The students sitting in the back of the room are giggling, but you don't know what they are laughing at. You ignore your upset student, but tell the giggling students to be quiet. You turn your back to write on the board, and all of a sudden a fight erupts in the back of the room. Your upset student is punching one of the giggling students repeatedly…

Could this fight have been prevented? Absolutely. In most cases, there will be a warning of violence prior to the violent act. Sometimes the warning happens only moments before the violence starts, but sometimes the indicators of violence could present several minutes before it happens. As teachers, if we can recognize these incidents and intervene before violence manifests, we have a greater chance of preventing a violent incident in our classroom. Below are some things to be aware of:

1. *Drastic changes in personalities. Has a quiet student started shouting? Has an outspoken student gotten eerily quiet?*
2. *Body Language. Humans communicate more through body language than with words. Pay attention to changes in breathing. Is the student staring intently at another student, possibly contemplating an attack? Watch their hands: Are they balled up in fists? How are they standing? Prior to a violent outburst, many people often blade their stance and adopt a "fighting stance" with one foot to the back and one to the front.*
3. *Listen to their words. Are they making threats or statements of violence?*
4. *Pay attention to rumors. Students sometimes plan a fight during lunch or gym and the word spreads quickly.*

There are many other pre-violence indicators, and all worthy of your attention. Incorporate these scenarios into your plan and mental role playing. Decide what you will do when you know a fight is going to happen, but has not yet occurred. Sometimes simply sending a student to the room next door is sufficient to diffuse a situation. Sometimes you may need to call for help in advance. Yet other times a simple discussion with each student involved individually may be enough to prevent any further escalation. In one of my schools, I had the guidance department on speed dial and often worked with them when I'd observe pre-violence indicators. I'd send one of the students to their office to cool down, or have the counselor come to my room to remove the student. The key is to do something immediately upon recognizing these indicators because the quicker you can intervene, the greater your chances of avoiding a violent outburst.

Self Defense

When it comes to self-defense against a student, each school, each district, and each state will have its own policies, laws, and regulations surrounding the subject. I am not going to encourage going "hands on" with a student for many reasons, liability being one of them. However, I am going to advocate for Teachers defending themselves against a violent assault from a student.

When a student gets violent, keep the following in mind:

1. ***Distance is your friend.*** *The more distance you have between an attacker and yourself, the more time you have to react and move away from such an attack.*
2. ***Barriers can buy time and distance.*** *If a student presents as if he is going to direct violence toward you, try to put as many objects as you can between you and that student. This way, if he does attack he will have several barriers to get through giving you more time to react and get away.*
3. ***Give commands.*** *Remember, someone is always filming. Tell the student exactly*

what you want him to do: "Get back! Get away from me! Don't come near me!" are all good commands to give. If it goes to court, you can testify that you gave clear commands for student to leave you alone as you tried to avoid a violent conflict.

4. ***Never position yourself so the attacker is between you and your exit.*** *Sometimes you need to get away, and you don't want to have to go through your attacker.*

5. ***Retreat.*** *There is no shame in running away. Although you may be capable or have the desire to stand your ground, the last thing you need is a YouTube video of you fighting a student in a classroom. Regardless of what led to the fight, it most likely won't end well for your career.*

6. ***Learn self-defense.*** *Regardless of how well you follow the above-guidelines and how prepared you are, there may come a time when a student simply snaps and attacks you. Whether acting in self-defense or not, swinging wildly against a student could cost you your job. There are many self-defense courses available that teach you how to quickly get away from an attacker. Many school districts also offer crisis intervention*

> *and restraint training courses for educators, which I highly recommend. They teach you what is allowed when it comes to self-defense and show you which techniques you are allowed to employ.*

Remember, it is impossible to predict, prepare for, or control everything that is going to happen. You may find yourself the victim of an attack, at which point you will have a decision to make. It is better to prepare for such a worst-case scenario than to decide on the fly what you are going to do. Although I do not advocate going hands on with a student, a teaching job is not worth your life or well-being. Even after employing all of the above-strategies, you may still be forced to one day defend yourself…

The Active Shooter

We have all witnessed the horror of school-based shootings in the media. Sometimes it's a student and sometimes a total stranger, but they all hold a common theme. An intruder enters the building with guns and sometimes bombs with the intention of murdering as many people as possible. As time passes, it seems these incidents happen more frequently and teachers find themselves wondering if tomorrow will be the day their school is targeted.

I wish I could present you with a simple list that would guarantee the safety of you and your students. Unfortunately, however, I cannot. But I will try my best to help prepare you to address any situation that is presented to you in hopes of increasing you and your students' chances of surviving such an incident.

As stated in the first chapter, you need to have a plan. As a part of the planning phase, you should be meeting with colleagues and administrators to review your school's response policy to intruders in the building. If you don't have a plan, you may want to take some time to develop one. Below is a sample plan that can be modified to fit the needs of your school. Please keep in mind it is not an all-inclusive plan and there will be elements that either need to be added or removed to meet the needs of your specific school.

Once an intruder has entered the building and the main office has been notified:

1. *A coded announcement is made (Code RED, Alert 1, etc.), indicating there is an intruder.*

2. *Students in the hallways are to immediately enter the closest classroom.*

3. *Teachers close and lock their classroom doors and cover any door windows with paper. The lights should also be turned off. Once the doors are closed and locked, they are not to be opened again. Remember: the identity of the shooter is unknown, and could potentially be another student who wants access to your classroom.*

4. *Barricade the door. If the shooter is able to gain access to your classroom, you want to make his entry as difficult as possible. Quickly pile desks and chairs in front of the*

door to impede a shooters entry into your room. This will not stop him, but it will make you and your students a harder target should he choose your room.

5. *Grab something to defend yourself with and prepare to fight. You and your students may have to fight for your lives. Keep in mind, if you find yourself in this situation, someone will most likely be injured or killed, but you have a better chance of saving lives if the entire class attacks the shooter than if everyone cowers in the corner. Chairs, scissors, or rulers: whatever you can get your hands on!*

6. *Teachers direct all students to a safe location in the classroom. Remember that bullets can go through walls and doors. During drills, I always place my students in the corner along the same wall as the door. Any geometry teacher will tell you that a shooter firing through the door will not be able to gain the appropriate angle to hit any targets in this location. Please keep in mind, however, that bullets can still penetrate certain types of walls, and that although I believe this location to be the safest spot in a one-entry square classroom, the shooter may*

fire randomly in the hallway and into those walls. With this in mind, I also have students get as low to the ground as possible.

7. *Take attendance. Teachers should record the names of all students present in the classroom. They should also note the names of absent students, students who left the classroom prior to the alert being sounded, and students who entered the room after the alert was sounded. This information will aid investigators in identifying not only the shooters, but also any missing students.*

8. *While in the classroom, direct your students to remain completely silent. The idea is to give the impression of an empty classroom so the shooter will move onto another target.*

9. *Cell phone policies will vary from school to school. In recent crises, students and staff have been able to call 911 and provide valuable information about the shooters to include identities, locations, the number of shooters, weapons, etc., which can help direct law enforcement to the threat and help save lives.*

10. *Remain in your room until given the all-clear or law enforcement enters to search the room. If law enforcement enters the room, stay exactly where you are and keep your hands visible. From their perspective, the shooter may be in your classroom. Minimize their stress by showing them your hands and not moving until directed to do so.*

11. *If your school has a security force or police officer assigned, they may be tasked with clearing the hallways. These are decisions to be made by the planning team and administration in cooperation with local law enforcement and do not directly apply to teachers.*

There are many more factors to consider, some of which apply only to administration and school security/police. For the purposes of this guide, however, we are going to focus strictly on classroom teachers.

As with the majority of this scenario, in many instances the situation will dictate the most appropriate actions for you to take, regardless as to whether or not they are in compliance with school policy. These are things you should spend time thinking about and planning for.

1. *What are you going to do if the shooter is in your classroom?*
2. *How will you defend yourself if the shooter tries to enter your classroom? Will you grab a chair? What will you tell your students to do?*
3. *How will you care for injured students? Do you keep a first aid kit in your room? Do you have first aid training?*
4. *If locked in your classroom for several hours, how will you pass the time with your students and keep them calm? What if someone needs to use the restroom or needs medication? How will you handle a panicked student?*
5. *Can you escape through a window?* ***Please keep in mind that sometimes there are multiple shooters, and escaping through a window could find you facing another gun or a pre-planted bomb.***

As stated previously, each scenario will be different and the situation will dictate many of your choices and actions. But take the time to plan and prepare. Have drills with your students and explain to them the reasons why they are hiding in the corner and lying on the ground. Reassure them that you are prepared for such an incident and they will be less likely to panic and more likely to follow your direction, which will hopefully result in the safe escape of all students placed in your care.

Additional Resources

Thank you for purchasing this guide and taking the time to review its contents. As a teacher and an author, my goal is to provide my readers with content that is not only useful, but also practical and easy to implement. In an attempt to offer teachers the maximum support possible, I have also created a list of free resources that will be periodically sent to your inbox via email for simply subscribing to our newsletters at the link below.

In addition, if you haven't done so already, I highly recommend reviewing Volume 1 of *The Urban Educator's Survival Guide; 7 Proven Strategies from a Successful School Teacher's Classroom.* This guide is also a quick read with excellent classroom strategies that are designed to help bring order to even the most chaotic classrooms. If you are looking for a more detailed description of teaching in a worst-case-scenario classroom, I highly recommend my memoir, *Service, A Soldier's Journey: Counterintelligence, Law Enforcement, and the Violence of Urban Education.* It details my experiences from Army Counterintelligence, to police work, to a violent Philadelphia classroom. Whether you want to prepare for a worst-case scenario in education, or learn how law-enforcement professionals and soldiers think in dangerous situations, this book is perfect for you. Get prepared today!

www.ServiceOfChange.com/Teachers

About the Author

Dennis Nappi II is a teacher, author, and advocate for education reform. In his free time, Dennis can be found gardening and hiking. Dennis is always looking for readers' feedback, experiences, and stories of positive change or success to share on his blog, Service of Change, and his Changecasts: Podcasts for Change. If you'd like to contact Dennis or learn more about his latest endeavors, he can be reached at the following locations:

www.ServiceofChange.com

http://www.Facebook.com/ServiceOfChange

Service@ServiceOfChange.com

Twitter: @DennisNappiII

If you enjoyed this guide, please consider writing a review at your favorite online retailer to help other readers find this guide and support our movement toward education reform!

www.ingramcontent.com/pod-product-compliance
Lightning Source LLC
LaVergne TN
LVHW010944110826
845149LV00013B/2752

9780991137541